SPEECH

000024

000025

SPEECH

Jill Magi

NIGHTBOAT BOOKS
NEW YORK

ISBN: 978-1-64362-007-7

Interior art: Jill Magi, courtesy of the artist

Design and typesetting by adam b. bohannon

Text set in Adobe Garamond

Cataloging-in-publication data is available from the Library of Congress

Nightboat Books

New York

www.nightboat.org

for Doug

CONTENTS

Introduction / She went out for bread

What does a man do with his words if they aren't useful for anything? He didn't ask that question, because he was walking, and his words were walking along with him, and breaking down with him and falling as if they were leaves falling from the branches of an old tree.

ELIAS KHOURY, from *City Gates*

To misplace
my notebook
I welcome

to vector
across heart-fields

pull unspun speech
drawing here
against there
diagonally, a world.

Reader, align
shoulder to shoulder
for prayers that stir
ideals and grievances

count borders
to cross out.

Sight-
less, speech is not
a measure of whatever
I want a savior a west
a north inside me.

What do women need
where a pair
has a grammar
where one and one make
their own form

where the root of
speech is to happen
is now and literature?

I walk to devolve
thick freedom:

warp tension
weft question

She went out for bread and on her way she walked past the open doors of the auditorium used for bridal gown, gun, and political conventions. She took some steps back and looked inside at floors being mopped in half circles. The mops like long hair sweeping back and forth leaving trails of water fading quickly under the lights.

"No, just looking. Thanks."

Until a man in a blue uniform closed the doors motioning for her to step back.

At the auditorium tonight the famous leader would speak and on her way back from the task of going out for bread she stopped again. On the other side of the closed doors she listened as he said,

"   not separate

                  when decency presses

      I am

                        what right to live without worry

                              some

      for food and for shelter   "

Birds nested on top of the walls dividing those who mostly worked with their hands from those who mostly worked at desks. Divided there and here, West City and East or South, held or contingent. Birds cackling over all of them. She pointed out this bird speech to the elder woman who replied, "wherever you go the gap is never silent."

The walls were concrete and thick like stone that might skirt an old city. One night she and others wrote the contents of the report on the walls and everyone read the labor. An attempt at public. A movement toward speech—like warm bread passed from one hand to another and from the walls nothing came back as the words made of chalk began to fade.

The walls were thick and reminded her of the stone walls that might skirt a city, writings carved into them. One night she would go and attempt that very thing hoping the clink of her tools wouldn't wake up the guards—the workers with passwords to all of the spaces but without citizenship.

One guard who never was able to sleep asked, "what will you write?"

"Quotes from Martin Luther King Jr.'s speeches on economic justice."

Turning away with a small shrug he let her.

So she did go and incise the walls with words that had been forgotten. In one version it was a script they could read. In the other version no one heard.

She explained:

"He was quoted on racial equality and not about class, the anti-capitalism parts of speech as if separate. Some white radicals dismissed him but he never stopped speaking economic justice never stopped ringing out the possibility—"

Outpost / _____

I propose an approach to studying citizenship and belonging that attends to the circulation and practice of multiple forms of governance in contemporary nation-states. This approach avoids exceptionalizing particular parts of the world and instead acknowledges that globally and locally circulating vocabularies of economy, belonging, and rights are assembled, disassembled, and reassembled *everywhere*. This approach does not disavow the specificities of different contexts, but rather resists thinking of them as anomalous, spectacular, or pathological […].

NEHA VORA, from *Impossible Citizens: Dubai's Indian Diaspora*

Is this version of city
to cross your outpost

a light blue gauze
a desert skin

a thick grey fog
a south side a redline

        is your outpost this
comfort version

your heart tent
your lopsided outpost

a crowded kitchen
a blocked window

blocked by too many beds
stacked for rent

is your north
crossing your south

dis-

        is your outpost a scratch
on this scene

or the Tuareg who guide you through
for your trust

or an architect who guides
a tour of paychecks encroaching

dis-

who do not talk to the intolerance
of heat the intolerance of votes

for segregation to tolerate
the weekend death toll

dis-

      who talks
to the cardinal other

the cardinal north
in notebooks thorned

saying come
be a better parent or wash up

your answers wash
up your pavement

      your outpost eye cross-
hatching looking at

who gets back on the train
gets back behind the gate

who wishes
the fence taller

wishes interpretation flailing
who stays away from you

who would be
the we of equal

        dis-

who watches fireworks
rocketing or pay stubs falling

glossing the memory of bombs
of fires set for profit

we
pitching the tent

at the start of the story
shuffling money

at the exchange counter
the men transacting in pairs

to better the chances of language
success or buying electric toys

cheaply for children
elsewhere home

        we
a part

sending the tale that travels
that maps a showcase

that we are not
here or there but trust

that everywhere
is a property

is a literature
a territory

So she asks
how comfortable are you

with indigo
billowing in a desert

who navigates you
through for a price?

He knows the water way and
draws the blinds down

draws down the veil where
if local is not a citizen

if I walk past
not the victim

and the sharp speech
in not conversing

the sharp of not
agreeing to be known

collapses the tent of betterment
of constitutional textbook

dis-

representation
a legal dis-

fiction for
if time and learning

buy my ethics
or if a theory blankets

a body with
a concept versus experience

lived
under siege or flood

a figure of them
makes a figure of rights

      then to go home
and allow your wife

we agree
to go home and disrobe your wife

we agree
to go home and vote for your wife

we agree
but a seminar for the needy elite

dis-

who make so much we don't see

dis-

who make so much so many deals

disto extract for progeny

dis-

good mother good father literate
living long and well

but never to read the ghosts they make
called swim or sink and shrug

do they know
who me?

Is my sovereignty linked to you representing me?

Do I think about sovereignty as I walk

as I write?

Am I free with my body or the state?

And so in which city did she go
as her speech could no longer complete

as poetry stops and starts
as through the alley a sliver

of car is seen a sliver of
not citizen seen

in the blue paint
of the sky above

seen in the tear
of memorial brick

in white plaster against the black
of shadows and grace

a city of shadows and grace
saying

      if the first tea is bitter
      as death the second tea mild

      as life the third tea
      sweet as love and

      if lightly your vectors line up
      over a bypass zone

      is love
      where lightly sands distribute

a border smudge
is love

for no idea is too stealth for wind
where the earth is so flat

for as a border does not touch
the ground

your speaking
is love

if she deeply laughs along and brings back
fruits sweetened in the sun

is love
if they wade out into waters clear

and if the gift is the relentless possibility
of the impossible

then you bathe
in a philosophical situation

where to clarify the fundamental choices
of thought

where to clarify the distance
between thought and power—

      and rest
      on that word power

where to clarify the value of rupture
we agree

        and so rupture may be
the ambivalent speech

of freedom given
or the sure speech of freedom

purchased
and rupturing the sky

she left from
and never fit inside

a freedom feeling
there

she walks
where the subject is not acting

is not an event or muscle
but is sympathetic

to the sphere of passion
of suffering of patience of

relation is susceptible
instead of immune—

        as here the slant built
places of worship

where impossible citizen
does not stop walking but

folds impossible glimpses
inside

not fully seen speaking
here joins the unfolding

pushing air up out
through enormous fans

   she, not the ultimate suffering stranger

   she, not a threat to the national order of things

and as treated window glass
reveals management lines

to order the faithful
in equality rows

she walks through a broadcast
through veins not

home
as light glows a niche

fueled by a tree
not east or west

as light doubles light
   impossible citizen lands

a job in a place eaten up by
origins

where the horizon
of who is who clears

keeps place where
they do not send speech out down the line

Not having their language
though they had hers

she kept place
              built a ceiling

below the ceiling
a door in front of the door

a window in front of the window
to the sky the hawk a visitor

to the silence of her desk
she spoke in the vestibule

preceding the vestibule
the door behind

the door opening up
time to think

              not in the grey of
a melancholy film not

the impossibility of language
or a book of lack

but to think in ripening red
without speech

              A change before a change she felt
the future of history forming

a cell wall attachment as
city inside the city

its cloud of secret perfume cresting
as black chiffon went walking

as suits filled with concrete
pressed forward

as uniforms parked their lookout
an impossible citizen does not ask

but following them
traces previous beliefs

as another wears the same fabric but minus
crystal flourishes lighting the hem so

tiny a detail lightnings her status
under them

       Under great leaders
projected on office towers

or leaders in hard hats below
beaming down flags that brush away dust

a flag inside the flag
a film of dust over the dust

over leaders in rows in storms of
cameras

she paused
remembering how they

create the below
and who must learn to love

so she saw the lens of the near
antonym of to learn

so insignificant she grew
in the year the dust lady pictured

famous as pathos dies
as the economy inside the economy

of no nets of
no health

brews a storm of
shame on shame

for what her country had

is

doing

So should she broadcast her
crestal tipping point

broadcast peace over peace as
a metal box inside the box

locked
the elastic truth?

      She placed a floor over the floor
went with others walking

to the market unimpeded by
a slip at the intersection

as the street interlaced
the people of whom

she was seen by and spoken into
languages luminous as bells

      as the clock beneath the clock
told the time

to turn decisions over
turn over every normal

right belief underwriting belief
to wake up knowing

abnormal coordinates
formed her own intersection

until sunset she
facing east

　　　　　facing speech waking up after
wake up America! and

somebody blew up
America its map

over the map
the true of the diagonal

across the south
of the north

　　　　　could this public script speak
as weight drains

as sand rushes out of pinholes
from her back

pillowing high above streets
above secret deals she realigns

her gravity her
supposed to—

floats

words

where a flush of speech would

where speech mixed with silence would

        Dear Union Sisters and Brothers,
not this solidarity speech

where if I am not him
then I do not deserve my happiness

is a whiteness speech
an exoneration attempt

where what is free
or not conducts

through wires dangling or
digging below to place

a public inside a public
wrapping wires around wires

like indigo patterns tied off
with string from

elsewhere as here
wraps tiny bundles around

there and there
is a fibral twining braid as

space between space is
when you know you do not know

all of what the central intelligence
agency has done in order to slant

a staircase that leads up into
a marble wall of

belief and back down
            the staircase binding

what she could see
to what she could not

afford and as her heat rose
she stepped out next to herself—

as the American Medical Association fatally weakened the drive for
socialized medicine by 1949, she locked the second lock of her door

as the attempt to revive the Fair Employment Practices Commission
was defeated, she went downstairs and crossed the street

as Citi-Bank lobbied for legislation to end Depression-era banking
reforms and won, she stepped up over the curb

as COINTELPRO dismantled the Black Panther Party, she lined up at
the stoplight

as the CIO expelled eleven left-led industrial unions in 1949, she paused
at the door that lead to—

as the federal government denied Marcus Garvey's UNIA a postal
permit, she slipped into the revolving door of the—

as Dr. King described "a lonely island of poverty" in the same speech as
"I have a dream," she made her way through the vestibule

as Rosa Parks trained at the Highlander Folk School and Septima Clark
ran a workshop on "Social Needs and Social Resources"

she put her card in the slot

as the Patriot Act was easily passed, she punched in numbers on the
private keypad and

as the First Pan-African Conference on Reparations was held, she
waited for what she called hers—

            and the list of who was shot
the list of who shot

came to her
over the air

as the list of drones
as the list of successful

statistics of hungers
as the list of states

of wars not so named
as the air inside air delivered news

as the news could not discern
what war from what peace

            an impossible citizen mirrors
the former place with a present

until she stops
her backward-look ticket

until one day how clear the air
as new heat

as old haunts
send history up her spine

twisting as vines
she kept place

sending figures away
with the others

in the air pressing transfer
over an ocean or more

as they climbed the curb
as the pavement sank

as the west pushed up
out of her head

everyone seeing the snake
breaking open democracy

    so it was never
your freedom idea

such a fragile skull ceramic
cracking with every them

with every
heavy axe of individuality

    the community cuts we agree

    the community mandates a training session
    on death we agree

    the community has its own mind and a ladder
    to a leader we agree

and these are not extra
thoughts like hair shorn off

for sale
like groups of men carrying new

blankets for shipments home not
extra like the boy crying

wanting new sneakers a mother
grabbing him shaking nothing

extra out
nothing extra

is not private
as the microphone clips

as the remote signals remote power
while the place for washing clean

attaches to the slant
clearly

      So further into indigo
she paused before the decay

the smell of death
holding border patterns

intricately holding her
blue was no home

inside her country
as the refugee is made

by universal liberty
as the refugee is made red

as a refugee makes her father
a feather shaking

the tether of foreign
making the code of local

as flecks of seeds in her throat
as her country and its heat rose

from green waters
cloth dipping its heavy shoulders

into the vat
            such was her skin

of not knowing and knowing
opening and stirring

her suitcase of privilege while she
over distance spoke

            "I feel close to   lost"

            while the seeds
to seal the color

grew next to the plant
used for dyeing

she learned this
comfort plan

complete blueprint
as the motor of night

brought thin promises
of slight sleep possible

inside her sleep
as cloth as skin pulled up

out of the water she
heavy with the oxygen

of listening of history lifting up
only to drop back down

on the pavement she crossed
with an exhale exposed to the light

of her beliefs turning toward blue—

sailcloth

questions

     kneeling

so this is beauty

       kenning

everyone sees
who is who

wave traveler for
refugee

wave traveler for
patriot

scratch universal
scratch it

write fear
over fear

stack table on top of table
desk underneath desk

and sit where
to be

is to sit
where the flick of a hand

keeps some at bay
beckoning others

from other tinted
windows from some

who squat
from some who stand

leaning against
a fugitive pose

from a window
that rolls up speaking

with so many pointer fingers
on a keyboard of elsewhere

making place
along with she

where if she said home this meant
no citizenship

        So with their status
they struck it and struck it

the screen around the screen
the profile snapshot laminated

cover sheet over
sheet and a shelf of books

behind a shelf
pulled apart by a zipper

      a mouth of teeth

      a mouth of teach

who learned
the shock of home stratification

the whitewashed layers
of so much speech

put into troughs
a satisfying feed

for policy secretly
to consign

      That life is not divided
into separate air-tight compartments

this was said in a speech
by the radical who lost

who knew
the book inside the book as

placenta apparatus discarding
the legible ethic only after

the birth of the lie of
easy rights for all

      "But if we cannot learn
from one another

what is right to think and feel
and do

then conversation
between us will be

pointless"
he wrote

      "relativism of that sort
is just a reason to fall silent"

as gladly inside those givens
she did

      feel the world as tiny particles. Not speech. A vast ear. Women
rose faintly. Still rose.

She stops and asks for bread from the oven for two coins. Networks
melt into the act of placing cool coins into his hand. She barely thanks
him. Light blue cuffs frame the contact of coin atop coin and the near
contact of two sets of hands passing and receiving a plastic bag filled
with warm bread.

Sign Climacteric

In the meanwhile, will someone who's going to the Climate Change Conference in Copenhagen later this year please ask the only question worth asking: Can we leave the bauxite in the mountain?

ARUNDHATI ROY, from *Walking with the Comrades*

Who dead told
who failed told

who no longer labors
who takes in chemically

so altered as to placate
the word syndrome

who studies fear who
sweats again sweats

to see the world swerve
who lives as lacuna asks

       do you remember her
whose skin papers who

soaks who disgusts who
beware cruel of youth

she
poured without spilling

smelted with no faults
drowning the knot of care

told who
wears a syndrome of climacteric

the antonym of apex
fallen into your gutter

rises ripe to cross out
the word produce

who pulls off the mask
who masks who

refugee patriot never individual
pathos unmaking liberty making

woman double woman who
publishes who profits who

tells the daughter who
finds her mother revolting

       I am not your mother
because daughter skin

thinks too much of loss
instead of the gain in

done the grain in

tilt   sift

float   fall

      fold,

      she entombs nothing
      that birthing body being

      folded into queer earth staging
      a party all night a strident

revolt
a flow away from

servile
supplement

Who young judges who
who empties while in

whose eyes
a gone grasp

        I know
without seeing her

she walks past who speaks
who enters easily

who exits easily
who lets the leash

of time fall slack
she

supple while rigid
because wisdom is not

who gifts but who savors
the edit of their demand

SIGN climacteric

SIGN see peri-
menopausal word

DIS-
appointment

INSIGNIA

see INSIGNIA body of meno-
pause imprints

DIS-

stench of over-stamping signage
lit up to see too much earth

to see what speech removal
tells

in surge
her heat turns

away from
away

mothers,

       tell me how to
       permission this

       swell
       edit out

       the child invisible
       give back gentle

       and care less
       if it shows

crestal crossover

epochal payoff

pivotal watershed

go-no-go fateful

quantal versus
words trending now:

pundit
tycoon
cudgel

        as between life and death
she experiments with

two sets of numbers
counting up or down

to environmental end
sinking planet skin

back into
placenta skin

into the glow of algal bloom
burning personal trouble

down from the inside
to the rough edge of

big ethics I turn
into you and away to come near

stitching memories of
childhood dreamlike

I know why they wrote
and now I will to remember

to increase peace to clear
the bloated choice of an individual

freedom legacy exchanged
for a sure system of making

that includes
giving away

young   womb

hoard   tomb

DIS-

her failing woman not
certified to be a self

today testifying her
speech of the change

speech as a claim as ripe
for murdering the service

of accumulating for him oh!
the dream of youth extracts

and drills out divides up
stashes away while

she knows how to kill
that boy that girl

to protect to protect them all
her arms

snaking
orchestrating

a climate change conversion
a dark indigo stirring she

laughs at the heat of certainty
her laugh gives it all away so

she sings—

> All for you, baby, all for you
> All for you, baby, all for you
>
> You took me out to the [inaudible]
> You took the hammer, you knocked my head
>
> You took the razor, you cut my throat
> All for you.
>
> I love you, baby, I love you
> I love you, baby, I love you

I'll take and send you to U.S.A.
I'll give you all the fine things you need

I'll give my precious life up for you
All for you.

You wondering if she
is true says

       hurl your eyes
       over the edge

       watch them roll
       tiny globes

       from the top of their game
       down into muck

       because you finally see
       you feel days as a soft brush

       back and forth
       on your brow linking

       this with that one side
       with the other

          take your lips
       hurl them into the trash pit too

       because now you know
       how to speak

everything reflects ancestors

everything an empty ear

everything her grey streaks is yours

       So follow oceans of pod leaders
allowed now to gather

the swarm to lead the song
       you can nest in her

logistics you can pick up
speed in her wake she

is a menopausal whale
it's true!

there are few who distribute
resources so evenly

whose curriculum of loss
teaches how to

DIS-

to go further
into the future with care

detached from progeny
to balance the last egg up

on her knee playful despite
toxic inevitability

to lounge with the spill
into the seventeen-mile crack

how to
DIS-

pull at nights not
dark

DIS-
inherit mothering

DIS-
inherit home

      sweet moon

      sincere thread

      slack line

      warping loom:

take back technology
who would force

a future shape upon
her own mother a full

paycheck as her heat
rose so free on one end

so tethered
on the other

       pulling site lines as string
dipping wick into oil

lighting a lamp for his death
she lit a lamp toward her own

       So what to teach is
flatness away from

authentic away from depth
the death of proof

the death of that book of faces
appearing as disappearing

       where what to teach is flatness
a need to surface all the reserves

in a stir of our sweat
a DNA tangle too impure

for screens
for maps

       At the airport
I watched her fall

and seeing myself tumbling
into age I ran to help her up

placing my palms under her arms
her sweat through silk flowing

into me
we blacked out together

never knowing each other knowing
everything

      You of too many days
teacher

walk away with their heavy
need her heavy need

to slice the scar off in
her retreat studio

her surgical theater
lets go of the gate

of the grid
to perform

      because too-clean skin
is not love she knows

as her forearm
tattooed with a feather

of blue
sticks to the seminar table

                as she tracks
their agendas

on chairs wheeling life-
less liquids around

windowless rooms
as her wet imprint

melts with time her
shame catering

to their spills until
DIS-

until her freedom is finally to know
their freedom was never for her

        "I can't translate myself into language any more."

                So she dreams of
a guaranteed income

she checks the facts of
this history

she thinks about this
guaranteed income

spoken by MLK Jr. then
and this research now

radiates into her and from her
the facts glide as she thinks this

would solve the polar ice caps
she thinks as she feels

how much poverty they ignore
how much they plant

ordering up surplus schemes
for so few

       as her heat of clarity rose
her heart electric

melted the whiteboard
blew up the tangled philanthropy web-site

finally sinking everything cute
sinking every market saying free

sinking her teeth into radical
ripening fur

       and the seventeen-mile crack
opened its gouge further

as pressed into paper she
felt their fear their heavy

shoulders paying
for their muscular

offspring who
so middle class

sopped up she
too OK with inequality

their young screens shut
their screens demanding

the violence in extraction
as we pledge to recycle

her scoffing at their easy
concern for pulp

        please put away your
moralism phones

and make
your own paper

DIS-
scantron

DIS-
office of hours and hours

of expression she yawns
swallowing them all—

to be held at the root
to be seen by the owl

flood the inbox with owls
press your sternum it sends

signals to speak and not to click
the box of a person to like

shelter owls in corridors
there are rooms filled with wings

talk in time when silence
in time when interrupt

talk in time when to clarify
shelters living time listening to

no record no retrieval
no archive no autobiography—

She walked away
out from under autology

into a net
of who applies blueness

into steady ever-night
re-

reinterpreting she, saying
"wings told me their layered ways"

Various East Various South

My goal is not to say yes or no to individual freedom and social constraint, the intimate event or the genealogical society. All I can hope is that by understanding how these discourses work to shape social life, we can begin to formulate a positive political program—something I have begun to describe as a politics of "thick life"—in which the density of social representation is increased to meet the density of actual social worlds. The goal is not to produce a hermeneutics of the Self and Other, but to shatter the foundations on which this supposedly simple relay of apprehension has historically established a differential of power as a differential of knowledge.

ELIZABETH A. POVINELLI, from *The Empire of Love: Toward a Theory of Intimacy, Genealogy, and Carnality*

Still the unequal
distribution of life and death

speaks still
stuttering the gap

between hope and harm
still an ear to the pitch

of endurance or
exhaustion which you?

An event broadcasts over
murmurs of chronic cruddy suffering

as she walks
across a parking lot

toward a home not
like a shared body

but a shared body
looping through

her black chiffon his white
linen his blue cotton her

uniform flowing an enfleshment
made mutual she touches

the string of theirs
pulling close to the beat of them

a soft spot in the bone
a cavity variously

inheriting a stress
a social constraint

a binding of not Europe
            while Europe says "their future

can never be a future"
the genealogical afternoon adhan

tumbles through the alley
between the pharmacy

and her skin shedding
its autology.

            Comes the green
afternoon window light spreading

making space she thinks safely
of her freedom tied to a man

whose coveralls
hang from his shoulders

in the sun whose fabric
of striped tape

reflects the light
around him as he works

in the median picking up
tissues

      how would democracy lift him
out of the heat

      how would absolute monarchy
lift him out of the danger

of traffic pounding
in two directions

she spins these
questions around him

      how would democracy lift her
out of home

where they ask about danger
until safety

collapses into charity
as a charity image

looks away never sees but
imagines his family

making the child to wake
for a school day

without him.
      So to accept

the pounding gift of funds
over wires she spies up

and they spy down at her
passing the labor bus

not allowed
in the museum parking lot

at certain times.
            Their not speaking

her ability to hear:
"the re-elaboration of self rather than

the identification of self
according to certain others

the re-elaboration of citizen rather
than the peaceful transition of power."

            She spins each mantra
alternating places

stashes them inside
her cloaked and authored walks

under the sun tracking
the parts that have no part

mapping an otherwise under the moon
its bright diagonal

sashing herself to herself
slashing the grid

      expert meanderer
      expert moon beam—

      "As morality has nothing to do
with measures of pleasure and happiness"

so network rip and repair
stitch up indigo and spin webs

repiece the dream of a golden
blanket of nearly invisible

exponential strength.
      This spider teaches how

woven you and he exist
outside official garments

where recognition
trembles—

      not seeing you
      not seeing me

wafting shining filaments
attached and free.

      Go tiny spider!
take your leap!

as I tangle in the web
of your temperature fluxing

it becomes me becomes
our indeterminacy

seals life itself to the we
walking once again in a state

of grace where if I cannot
spontaneously interpret you then

I do not draw
a red line through.

When the light turned red
she brought the housing project

into her thoughts
through her mouth

making a city
making her

a memory called something Green
to denote the garden it wanted to be

where they desired to stroll and sit
but learned how to

keep on how to
cut out

cut up
masterfully.

I mean we swallow all
at the light green

cars pull off highways
to pick up drugs for fun we know

the news drives back to the suburbs
we know the report provides

a number of those shot dead
their person being a weekend

elsewhere
being days off—

      recreation link death

      disposable income link death

      extra time link extra death

      fun days

      not knowing

that whole economies
reject repair.

      So to call a town friendly
draw a dotted line

below your neck below your
smile is a school district

a real estate name
redrawn

renamed
so as to drain

for profit
for one idea of fun

      urbanism
      a tourism

I mean to say that most
do not believe in equal

and will advocate for less
versus their progeny more—

So take a hospitality vote
take a friendly bike path

go south to edit out
a beach integrated late

take the girls wading out
their joy a lake a task force

goes beyond the buoy
the sum of one idea of skin.

Take the cost
of containing the south side

the west side versus
the clink of gallery glasses

a tinted window
art, a school,

paving the way
to pay for it.

Drop me off at the station
drop me off at the line of the lake

to cross against the wind when
comes a group of three teenagers

and the question
"how will you get home?"

asked at a poetry reading
of fixity.

      We, a difficult commute
reading a stack of bills reading

impersonal policies impinging
on a person I do not know

the boys their mothers
and how easy it is for guns to purchase

a city where bodies
make a zone to cross

      we, a whole lake of grief
repeats where the bereaved

comfort the bereaved
salty water seeping into

the foundations of a city who
insists on friendly.

      Now push the line up
push the refusal

while if all I have
is to see

then this will I say:
a lake sits on a map

a gulf sits on a map
a picturesque skyline gives

teeth to a boat tour
for architecture to float through

the economists and their theories
who calculate and wash up

tinder on shores elsewhere south
elsewhere east

while the shine is built
to keep looking up.

       Pick it up, skyline looking good
pick up the folded policy

coming clean
big lake, big gulf, wide hem

under polite cover
untuck innocence

blurt, claw, stumble
away and invert the world

for a small hand of grief
to hold it is yours:

a zone marked by patrol
a north zone of smooth hair

and publicly drunk allows
a south zone to publicly pay.

She sat in front of the dents in the reed of the loom
through which she pulled "repeated exposure to so-called everyday

violent crime" and separating strands of the warp, she pulled the study
"Police-Recorded Crime and Disparities in Obesity and Blood Pressure

Status in Chicago," making the motion that would hook the strand again
and again "and perhaps even help to answer that oft-asked question

that she—and likely many other Chicagoans—field when they travel:
'Is it really as bad as all the news says it is?'"

She pulled the sentence "The violence was also extremely concentrated"
through the next dent and through the next she pulled "Network Science,"

"how the connections between people, organizations, and places affect
what we feel, think, and do," and through again she pulled the idea

that these connections "affect whether or not you get shot" and as she heard
the researcher say "While network science does not address problems

with poverty, education, and unemployment," she pulled the last thread—
thereby threading the loom upon which she walked, shuttling across her city

preserving the weaver's cross, her freedom and opportunity analytic falling
slack and pulling taught, making a pattern alternately bounded and not

by the frame of her front door.

Then I saw sunlight
fill empty lots
shadowing

as a bus trip moved me
into the next town
of factories emptied out
of shingles missing but not
laughter at the depot

grandmothers at the depot
new kicks fresh white shirt
jeans carefully creased
in open space and light

too much too many
direct hits in such open ranges

and like blood
upon hearing "bullets" I flow
away from the invitation
to bleach out the stains, from
networking clean and predicting
everything but the cause.

So I take my apology labor
get back on the bus.

Take the side door
push the vector down over a trend
slide along the statistical row.

Burn down the personal
reseed the want of reassuring smiles

fold safety back
into the search for a system

where a study is not a singular pose
as it feels for the roots that make
a self a city a country sink
under the great spine of democracy
the great glow of a crown.

SPEECH a lake of lack
of desert valves
of the haves and not—

SPEECH another country
cloaked in no citizenship
where the relentless SPEECH
of a blue sky shows me
how systematic ruin
continues to continue
to like to check to vote.

000016

000018

000017

000019

Until she hosts,

In *Al Madhafah*, Hilal [...] will host visitors in her apartment space on campus. *Al Madhafah* is inspired by the Syrian refugee Yasmeen who turned her living room at a refugee camp in Boden, Sweden into a space where diverse people can gather. For Yasmeen and her family, the act of hosting subverts the role of guest and host, giving a political and social meaning to the living room space. This act is a powerful claim that Hilal calls "the right to host."

SANDI HILAL, from the flyer for
"Al Madhafah: The Living Room Performance"

To read the sidewalk
under the sidewalk

always shred the carbons
the dangerous between

how document atop document sees
reads the religious book re-typed.

       She holds the thin pages
book of carbon letters

blue artifact disallowed
       but this is already written

so turn the page
to the sound

of a dry new migrant.
       Her fingers imprint the pages

of a country invisibly
its pages of disobedience

a limited-edition danger
doubling.

       The blue code fades
so to forgive—

so he forgets
so she writes

until she hosts.
       How she knew to shred

the trace to hide the splicings
all her life until in a new city

she would succumb
to illegibility

its open room for others.
   In the sun the blueprint fades

into a guest who hosts
a memory of childhood

a pastel façade
over which she rose turning

to a giving sun
raking the walls of chalky

concrete making
soft her new living room.

   Count the volumes weary
from the title *Home and Exile*

and *The Writer as Migrant*
carried in protective cases

set them off in tiny boats
and count—

   no more romantic nomad.
Then what book? Then why tarry if

it's better on the other side?
Then to invite who does not belong—

she crosses the street
over the need to difference

to count between refugee and patriot
she presses send as a father

releases his arrival.
          Count images on Al Jazeera

who says Europe again Europe
heaving tightening the bindings

ratcheting up the boundaries
of more big books. This is how

over-tired arrives.
Count—

          how love comes up out
of the ground underneath the pavers

the pavers of unsettling down
into sandy abstraction

sandy necessity—
          but food is not abstract

so revolution feeds on hunger
so she mines the spread

of dis-margin lava
as a global flow meets the sea

knowing that something new
from this heat must be.

Ever-guest, unseen, arrives
at the poetry event where

"No one wants to hear your opinion
on politics, bedroom, leaders."

So write the bed
under the bed your politics inside

your poem a poster sleeping
in public under your visa blanket

sleeping under the scan
inside the scan a secret word

wrapped in a secret page
tucked under the rustling

of official papers.
            Substrate under substrate

arrives in the form of a casual shirt
a form of grammar ease

the ambassador stands
to take a small bow

at the performance
where the west of the crowd

cheers for their favorite beach
an impression of citizenship lodges

a vote for a shopping mall
as another form of love

from over the ocean
slides under this silence flag.

      I slipped there also, saying,
"I would never   that   writing"

where whispers of going away
is how to stay, saying,

           "I don't disregard love underneath love
               I don't turn the official down

        but I know the roots of another place where speech
           swerving and wild gets used next to me

           out of me. Where the slam in slam
               is the myriad is violence
        in order for new wordplay new worlds—

               I've said some things.
        Now take a break from the mouthpiece."

Into my mouth I put
eating cheaply into
my mouth a condominium
able-
bodied enough to climb
up to a balcony

into my mouth I put the view
from above into my mouth
my eyeglasses
until my tongue
in slivers

into my mouth
the cursor disappears
so I must guess where
I am in this glitch field
in which the refugee
won't fit

she stopped being my father—

because the farmer
hung himself
another also as
I open my mouth
and another won't stop killing
won't stop crossing over
for my mouth to be
full for agribusiness to flower
out of my poetry lips

a bracket
a code

a beautiful throat
swallows the map
of our paychecks
of bauxite of coal
of transactions
as that one and that one
over there earn a different
rhetoric another poetics

while managers
paste and present learnings into
my mouth I put
metrics
metered and voiced

rubrics of
how to open up
markets for cheap food
cheap cloth

for gags to sound
the security alarm
of error-
free speech.

Who is she?
      in whose eyes

white white double
never new never novel

because in the time it takes
a father certain of only English

to arrive as white
her certificates

scrape this place off.
      She leaves the peelings

of her movement up
the globe

in her office of hooks
for hanging badges

their promises of entry
place pressure on her sight.

      She notes pieces
of vision gone missing

going never further
toward being seen

as the grey she has become
her body a screen

of knowing and not—
        preparing substrates

in sets of two
sanding down blue so as

to apply more blue
        she materializing

as open book
its double-page spread, she

        an impossible citizen
at the always airport where

a hand over the counter
receives her passport from

a hand placed
over a mouth agape.

        Yet never before
had she so much time off

from fear
        so she watched

as the gate after the gate
closed on children left behind

remembering a taller friend
the gates closing

on his brother shorter
because a mother must choose

which son
because limited arrival papers

limit the mouths
shortened by a lack of milk

a lake of difference.
          Who is she?

white doubling
up her health chance

dumbing down her sight
an over-built decision

a subject over-
told and why the multitude

can never be represented
so riveted to the image

of a mother, she
we agree went bravely.

          Who is she?
Between mother and mother

a city presses down
a document forms another skin

between a country east
and another direction felt

as her clavicle balances both
north and south

east and west
son other son.

There is a city where
some buildings

take the shape of tents
some come down

in piles of concrete
but continue as gathering spots

for the men
who used to live there

where windows repeat
where they wear the same pants

the same shirts who walk
inside memories of

water and salt
thick sunrise thick

morning after morning in
emplacement rooms of

unruly wallpaper
new photos old frames

crumble mobility
to raise it up again

to send it over wires from
a city heavy with currency—

            weeping woman
who is she?

pressing the button sending
a waterline mark a tee-shirt

for sale reading, "I love _____ because
someone in _____ loves me."

            A mother opens a new atlas
a grief atlas or

what if she is OK?
And he? What if new?

If relief?
The affect anthology

will not hold this alley inside
the alley the sprue

to a heart
that pours out

a new day, she
a soft laugh at the office, she

a picnic, or shopping, an ordinary
weekend, she

free of family each week
a decision pulls her forward

to walk out further into the tides
to rise up

out of bed for work further
without the children

without this father
without this mother

who press send
whose toy sounds fade

around the corner
from gold promises—

      exchange city for city
hold compare against compare

saying, "I left our victimhood
at the bottom of their steps."

If we stood apart from conjuring up some future

if purposes were achieved in the very moment of expression

if this was within the reach of anyone who desired it

if the present is a site of freedom

if nonviolence is an epistemological quality

if morality is located on the battlefield or in duty

if fearlessness is the essence of all virtue

because aristocratic forms of ethical life

depend on luxuries like time and learning

because innocence denies art

because every person is thinking

    then the roof from which he fell was art

    then the exhibit was a comment on labor

    then he fell while sweeping dust

    then he followed the artist's directions

    sweeping making a shimmering veil for us to see the sunlight

    until his weight

until the ceiling the artwork gave way until he fell

then the exhibit actualizes a pain concept she did not intend

as artist to heal and he as worker to author.

Some Various West

If Gandhi's vision of nonviolence is to be taken at all seriously today, we ought to acknowledge that one of the great challenges facing its proponents is to think about what a "citizenship of the world" might look like that does not invoke the rights of man as its justification. For unlike rights, which can only be guaranteed by states and are thus never truly in possession of those who bear them, duties belong to individuals and cannot be stripped from them.

FAISAL DEVJI, from *The Impossible Indian:*
Gandhi and the Temptation of Violence

"Risk writing into the problem."
Twice she did

twice the verve of youth
writes a letter to the editor

so sure
of rights where speaking ricochets

off rib and femur
then sinks in its ink—

   Therefore if the newspaper
says so many infractions were labor

then whose pay?
whose protest

sails in from elsewhere
eager for this news

for the region receives
the overblown secular

measured out in doses
of official speech—

    news as other
    scratch on it.

So implicated in a cleaner art
she thinks of the men

who all press send who
cares to read

the waterproof banner who
says "art"

who dips down
into the city of always

plunder or savoir, which?
        how to plunder

here and there:
        do you see her

not speaking in your own city?
Woman declaring climacteric

pinpoints your geography
never as only your own.

        As she mirrors them
they sail in with strong arms

sleeved in simple ideas
sweeping diasporas up

rowing across
world bank impact

with the force of enlightening
a better day

always someone else
to pay

      as her electric silence
asks, "What are you doing here?"

answers, "Rowing enlightenment
against brown people"

in a regular meter
in a tradition against

a veil a stripped
progress imprint

returns the news
of the news of betterment.

      This book
its fissure its freedom

presses release
on the simple button

as water works its way down
into the other city

where they puzzled over her arrival
a stranger of white walking

in on territory guidelines
where private police badges

nod her through
to an enclave is a university

declaring its right
to know.

            Who walks into the hills
where revolutionaries occupy

who is deported or shot
for roads for mining

as inroads come
hailed as progress

for hauling off the wealth
            as a presidential visit

in whose skin
has the developing

world arrived—
Which you?

            Under the forest is a forest
under your electronic progress

statement under your elected
protection statement until

crone
until your knowledge of this

never leaves
knowing corporations are not

abstractions and an island
for high culture under development

crosses out rights
until the rights commission returns

tossing skulls over walls tossing
burial ground pamphlets into the gap

between the federal building
foundation and sand

emptied and full of bones was
another city

       which island?
       which grid?

       More than saving
more than winning the debate

more than investing
in the hills where mists cover

the truth
of what is mined—

a tree saves
itself easily

while knowing this says
       "I walk to devolve thick freedom."

                Meanwhile
at the institution everywhere

inside the room
of miniature thrones

everyone takes a seat
to put in their pocket

                she patterns who
will not read her

but that is already written
so start over

                meanwhile
at the institution everywhere

men white men write
the labor problem

on which they lecture
as new experts in the common

area tonight
in the form of one microphone

as rows of chairs
focus us on not speaking

as everyone signed in
on clipboards signed up

for the paycheck
down in the common room

and on the way
to the upper floors

later saying, "that was fun"
is an economy of too many arms

snatching up another study
their purses of discomfort

make work to clean the others
their purses of study open up hungry

as "I don't know you" comes
crashing into a dream of what is mine—

and as Dr. King began his speech at the March on Washington
for Jobs and Freedom, she tied her sneakers

as he criticized class systems that segmented America,
she put a small towel in her bag

as he incorporated women's welfare rights into his 1968 agenda,
she opened her front door and locked the two locks behind her

as an anticommunist fanatic stabbed Dr. King in Harlem in October 1958
nearly killing him, she pushed the elevator button and stepped inside

as Kennedy delayed fulfilling his campaign promise to equalize
federally assisted housing

and the SCLC inaugurated Operation Breadbasket to address the crisis of
joblessness, she got off the elevator and opened the glass door of the gym

and as King's visit to India solidified his anger at poverty and imperialism,
she pushed the button to start the treadmill.

000020

000022

000021

000023

This steep repeat —

So I want to argue, or move in preparation of an argument, for the necessity of a social (meta)physics that violates individuation.

FRED MOTEN, from *The Universal Machine*

To pack and go quickly
while others ship boxes

for the next generation's
object relief

for stability constructed
from cheap iron bookends

one still life unframed
one family Bible

a worthless vase
and speech as marble pillars

elsewhere
       this steep repeat—

       "Don't you point your finger at me!"
said at the border as it spits up

this sharp mother this
impossible mother speech

while he thinks through rights
where "always peaceful is a polite choice"

political and stamped
she listens

thinks
"If you had one hour

you would go to the bank
to close an account

to withdraw all and who
does not? Or who plans? Haves?"

While an impossible citizen thinks
that others also felt pain yesterday

over her shoulder
this book follows her with

no speech as she walks
she thinks that others

grieve also a fence
a diagnosis

a sudden phone call
or slowly the news

presses into the nation
underneath the nation

the war under the war
presses against the door

behind the door
into the person who is

two maps
at once.

At the base of society she finds the base of her skull. Her superstructure waits for shifty instrument feedback until a father went refugee status for her to say, "there I can say anything I want. This has weight. Was home"—

His slouching historical back his bones as feathers their secret fissures ask, "did you know there is an organization determining how free is your country? Check your rating fluxing."

"Whose country? Which you? Whose heat?"

"Not the refugee with his pants unzipped his pants short. Messy tourist go loud and others stealth. Messy citizen goes loud or who makes themselves small in public space or wanders freely looking up."

Say hello to the gap in her dictionary a gap in her blouse. To cover this up and stop speaking in such an accent she never learned his tongue. To cover this up his too many arms. All the hands to cover up his gaping accent.

What is the code for a small family on a street hovering over a baby without food over the baby's last bottle? Who is programmed to want and want to see and to see?

She stays with the baby while he goes to find food. Their backpacks snag the screen of pity snag donations that delete barbed wire delete bodies in line.

Who is not pictured who is left behind where the siege follows the
edges of buildings. Not running in vectors not the drama of open-air
choice. This image of a single file her child following closely behind.
Who guides them through waiting at the intersection is a body bent.

What if
refugee? Can you curl

into smaller?
Strategy of many

necessary for empathy
to quickly

release and flee
when later comes grief

when the heat
of the quick melts

into the long silk of loss
Will you thrive wanderer?

What your speech will be?
Later

or now
is literature

please package your
our theory

not too wet please
our tissues have not caught up

with your refugee
we agree theatrically—

The mother pulled the box of important papers out of the refrigerator.
A prisoner mother is not impossible. Late afternoon the door behind
the door knocks. Nearly kills. This repeats

      while with disposable income
I spot a refugee

at Europe's freedoms and borders
eating and eating

      She was my father as time slips
from my new nomad satchel

as time laughs at his short pants
at this wet book

      the book always she
always wrapped in bandages

for the new cold for the
new sorry for sorry

to make any mark beyond
victim keeping you impossible

      Who so clean
so made of goodness?

      Europe delicious and narrow
made of refugees made so narrow

an idea for us is them
to slip between

      "I touched history easily there"
said as she stepped in front

of the line of refugees who
has a red passport

or papers fraying
a rough folder

who is escorted into a grey room
built out of edges

where the sound of shoes on tile
is history

is always an airport
always in the tone of voice of uniforms

      Until slither out small snakes
from the extra papers

a family holds together
not meant to hatch yet

as the passport inside the passport
heats up the hope of skin to stay contained

until permission stamps
their autobiography out—

I wrote and wrote their loops
until my pages were covered with
efficient plastic eye scans
and I stopped penning this
about the north and south city everywhere

knitting
razor-wire networks

writing progress
as the snarl that it is

I went up a globe
to the sea inside the sea
the shore upon the shore
and back down
to the spread of policy
of poetry sorry so polite

and I stopped penning this.

Now at the same time
I felt rapture

standing in front of the gold grids
tiles radiating only gold

and tiny lines between and between
every image always in two.

      I could barely claim this double joy
my heart in halves

so much so that I only want flatness—
      please withhold your trick of depth.

I was in that marble city of
purple-grey light

across east and west
where another empire was once basking

as a church as a mosque
and I settled into ancient steps

marble threshold depressions
from the weight of stepping

over so many years.
      The evening glided over me

sending its low light across walls
ablaze with the memory

of the digital.
         I felt the touch of flatness

as the call to prayer went swelling
its light finally bleeding out progress

over two seas
over rolling seas.

        I tumbled with this golden light.
I climbed the ladder

back to the concrete time of the present
a ladder a rib cage

        repeating, "window, mirror,
stone, and gold."

I climbed the ladder and saw
the bones of a border

streaming people
and then I saw the stamina

of my border my mettle
"to speak"

        each column a throat
each peak my spine doubling

my skin twice
a magnet for historical heat

testing my easy love of purple
in a city skeletal asking:

      how do I write "explosions"
      "I am not from Syria"

      or "This line for anyone
      with an Iraqi passport"?

She sat in front of the dents in the reed of the loom
through which she pulled the August 1953 CIA-sponsored coup

against a democratically-elected Iranian government, and separating
strands of the warp, she pulled the 1911 Anglo-Persian Oil Company

pumping oil out of Iran through, and in the same way she pulled CIA agent
Monty Woodhouse through, making the motion that would hook the strand

again and again insisting that international communism was a threat
to the West, as she subsequently pulled the one million killed

during the Algerian war of independence through.

She pulled Italian colonial rule in Libya through and through again
she pulled the jailing of the leader of the Tunisian Doustor party

and through the next slot she threaded Britain's actions against Egypt's
Wafd party, finally pulling the 44 percent share of the Suez Canal

that Egypt sold to get rid of debts to France and Britain through the
next slot as Britain installed the Sunni Hashemite King Faisal in Iraq

in a heavily Shia population in 1922, and thus she pulled the sectarian
schism that would tear Iraq apart after the American invasion of 2003

through the next space in the dent of the loom, as the two great
confrontations of the late twentieth and early twenty-first centuries

were slotted next: the Cold War and Islamic extremists—she pulled the
CIA's covert action against the Soviets in Afghanistan

through the next slot in succession.

She sat pulling the words from Benazir Bhutto addressing the first
President Bush in 1989, "I fear we have created a Frankenstein

that will come back to haunt us," as she pulled the overthrow
of the moderate Pakistan People's Party government in 1996 through

and as Prime Minister Sharif praised the Taliban and promised to
emulate it, she pulled the last thread—

thereby threading the loom upon which she walked daily shuttling
across her city, preserving the weaver's cross, her freedom

and opportunity analytic falling slack, making a pattern alternately
bounded and not by the frame of her front door.

Now words float down. See the gentle of that.

Good or bad, I'm happy to welcome both.

I don't hear with my ears, I don't see with my eyes.

A voice speaks inside my heart,

My jewel-lamp burns bright even in a rampaging wind.

from *The Poems of Lal Ded*, translated by RANJIT HOSKOTE

I would look up from this work, put gardenias in my hair.

She who shuffles I

stirring my bag for an inventory of what spills—

I would garden the vines

turning from my roots, my internet

twines.

Is this which continent? Is this the tap of fingernails on a keyboard?

That's not speaking. So feminine, so deferred.

Some say anything in speech is an event.

Council housing windows: can they speak? Where eyes canyon the daily news. Applause in the rap-battle courtyard. Some say that's not here not speech enough.

Or listening to resist practices, batik being one or if you tie your tongue as string around bundles of fabric so hacking the engine of speech.

The Futurists over there doing something to the library tour guide. Stop
their mauling but they will start again at another historical intersection
despite protect despite rights.

If an artist

If I put lemons on a plate and paint

that would
my speech be

If I protest

This is why art
not always

posters

So carry my dividing line with me
then speech makes sense

of what is not said
such as mahogany-paneled rooms

repeating privilege
on one side of a city

making the other. This class
room repeats broadcasting

its paneling murmurs
its progeny mirrors

its secret how-to—

I wrote about speech
but did not know the memory

of workers attempting
to cross the highway

in the seam of sunset
and headlights. They lean

against guardrails until.
I watch my breath shallowing

as they billow their shirts
in shifts behind a fence crossed.

I look again and see them sitting
peacefully on the embankment

of the other side in the sunset
of a normal evening

conversation. A group
wades out into the mangroves

memorizing the hidden roots
of a day off.

So this watching means
I reject speech class

where over-teaching combs away
the mistake where the video shows

where I should start
middle and end

I want the tricky nets
please give me all the tricky nets

because safety envelopes speech goers
who can pay for the curb

to cross safely
to hold their morals by

the stem of the glass
and sip in vestibules

where serving trays deliver speech
deliver an identity of ideas

and why I won't practice the headset
their too-many arms

because my ancestors
won't fit.

      Still to be paid I partake
in their public relations until

my smooth muscle rejects
until a nasty little nibble

on the finger pointing.
      Still to be paid

I stay outside as I walk inside
and share a claim

to taste to fold
along the seam for to teach

and read the impossible
is to know

the possibility of the multi-
logic—

        look under the study
perform the ableness not to belong

stop and wander
cast a lazy net

poke holes
in the nativist curtain

dig a passage to a province
inside of me to upturn

my own containers who would write
a biography of rights—

"If I disagree using my speech
while moving toward you

If my skin disagrees with
our rights—

If you choke
on my speech

If I choke
on your body

If I exist
disagreeing moving toward you

If you snap my edge

Then the risk is living

where to be
is a risky quote."

The archive first
was family

how she corruptor kept place
out of place

making a portable horizon
from the diagonal

her fingers pulling the thread
the ontology of mistake

where she set up a laboratory
political so refugee so

to step off
the curb of guidelines

the curb of a sentence
she drew a roving across

her body snagging
the grid of

official family
patriot archive

drawing a feather
as father

in code

   in total   a system

shouldering

      being almost

dead   stepping over

      citizen non- or

DIS-

      liberty   anti-

body

      his papers naturalized

and lost

      learned her   then

how to

      "a man without a country"

weave

Now words float down. See the gentle of that. In his office retyping
through sheets of carbon I live this carbon. He clicks away at my art
surface letting us be citizens his fingers still click, typing.

Thin paper floats between us and others may wonder what can be taught. I wonder also. They wait for certain speech but I am inclined to withhold until—

        because the partial is a trap
and not knowing pulls

at the fabric of the South Side
or asks

who in class
can report back to an official.

Real is also
I need a nice dress not on credit

is not a violation
of what my mother taught.

        Writing not using a pen.

        Logos over-
        valued.

        Painting
        scripting.

What if flatness
is an ability to love?

       Not to decide
what is next to say

or authentic
       only recopy existing texts

to transmit the distance between
speech and power.

Now pieces of paper float up.
I don't understand that.

But they keep floating up and up
in this wind that unsettles the unbuilt area.

      If this city is not a daily diary
then papers float up blank

fluttering all the small cameras
as "my perception matters"

finds itself lonely
and surveilled oceans away

      while some minarets
were made to shake

in earthquakes. Some
razed because of rights. Some

conversations listened
into softly. Some virtual pages

all lift up. Seismic and blocked.
Entire pages purchased and rescinded

as an information corporation eats and eats
as we feed it an idea of freedom

a satisfied uplift
      or if recopying is to author then

everyone walks out from under
the library scratching keys against

the vitrines saying
"Let's revamp protocols of inquiry."

At the antiques souk he would not sell the book to me. Because of the
wrong religion I was allowed to see the writing inside and not to touch.
I asked why without access without touching. Closing its covers he
answered, "we are a tolerant people."

If you are a vector without access.

If painting and the desire for color crushes.

If the vector once the poem now

painting as
bibliography.

Painting a bibliography.

Burying narrative under color
under love story under object. Just now finding its shades.

A lens for watching the skies change.

You go quietly into a garden.
A fence of beauty guards against speech, lets

speech in. Both ways.
About a place I do not know

I will never hear the argument so surely again.
This speech.

Meanwhile, the correct
waterproof banner speaks

infinitely sturdy against the direction
of the script of some wronged.

I watch the survey economically
made into art

correct
compass

begin to stick to every finger
who displayed their

not west toward
the directed and progressive

white clean and
sponsored screens—

"Brother, Sister
give me wrong

give me
a delicate pinnacle
not to achieve
political

give me low-
scoring speech
who makes a look

inward
homeward."

Nor news nor strife

could hold her love of flatness

nor the solipsism of political poetry

written by her love nor

her new love of purple-grey

and golden light the pieces lining up

as shallow breaths in patterns

against her skin in patterns set

into the wall that held the dome

a great lung moving her through

the sunset through fourteen centuries

of stitches moving through

the silk of his fingers

In this time they touched

a dusting of yellow and marigolds blooming

around snaking stones everywhere

giving up the battle against grief

they shuttled through history

a push out of obsessions with clear skin

with clear cause through into the corner store

of laughter under the thick evening

the men and their laughter unraveling

whole lengths of loss

How important to hear this song

to see the child carried on her hip

carried underneath so many folds

They put themselves into the air

of seeing and took in the bitter

and sweet gift of knowing that pain

would continue like water in ripples

and that they would never capture

the clearing nor the design of happy

So they tidied their house

and sent away the broken dishes

from an era when their debt was all

they could read

They were not alone as the sun

blended their shadows with others

across passport lines

flying across strategic targets

a murmur of life spoke

in the warm spot under her arm

the child found a nook a burrowing

as they remembered their travels

on raging vectors when they never saw

the ground swell so tuned in

to what was due—

subway fare grocery bill rent—

to hide the struggle for the shame

Then to disorder this history

to corrupt the script they came home

to clean the rooms they built inside

the given rooms the windows in front

of the windows to see further despite

the news of flags of failures to spread

the sense and fiber inside speech

never to be un-pulsed—

Post-Script / A Third Space

Two cities of middles overlapped inside my notebook. This was confusing though I was not unhappy. Until heat rose up in me and I went from asking, "where should I live?" to thinking, "here I have something to learn" which was to believe in poetry's making despite the misrecognition, "poet equals citizen," as if a poet could only be real through official belonging. In fact it had always been the opposite.

So I went walking with the others who vector across parking lots, alleys, and through city blocks where there is no set path. From my window I watched their movements as if they were stitching new embellishments into the city's surface. Then I joined them making curves and diagonals. Without speaking, carrying my notebook in a canvas bag: city and me, sweating and absorptive. Over and over to step off the curb—tiny leaps—into the mix of watchful communication between me and the others who walk, between the backs of buildings and alleys, between me and drivers who yield and to whom I signal "thank-you" by placing a hand over my heart.

This is what I heard: Who is she, walking here? How is she a guest and who does she host? Does she walk comfortably with history and the world? What couldn't keep her at home? What is her language? Or I heard nothing at all, feeling disregard, nonchalance, the absence of curiosity directed toward me. My own voice rang out sharply then.

Susceptible, I took in the questions and silences. I composed an essay on "writing in an elsewhere" and made a project called "Last Book": stacks and stacks of the same stark white book without title, author, cover art, publisher's imprint. I said I was quitting poetry until I remembered my refugee father (who called himself a refugee when we made fun of his mismatched clothes—"Don't make fun of the poor refugee!"—and we would laugh) who unintentionally taught me what poetry is for. His seat in the living room where weekly he hosted guests after church and I watched, shocked by his confidence to do so. I began to imagine hosting others which is to speak. Which is not necessarily to belong but how to live with longing.

With a listening ear I saw the former place more clearly in the new place; this clarity made a third space which was more like a method and less like a site. Not speaking *for* a place *I wrote out of place*. Toward the cities and people ambivalent about my permanence and my art—those who have been, incidentally, the most generous of teachers.

Painting a bibliography.

A feather, a brick, a twig. What are they doing in this book?

On my walks I occasionally bent down, picked one up, and slipped the new relic into my bag. These objects sat near my writing desk and as *SPEECH* stopped and started I began to paint their likenesses always floating and flat: fugitive-like. They have no shadow no weight and no context. Placed on square substrates usually in a set of four they refer to the grid of weaving. And as weaving measures the passage of time while material accumulates, so do the paintings. Textilic, both. Hence the idea to stamp each painting with a number in sequence.

Each numbered painting does not index a complete thought though the object painted appears to be revered. Perhaps the paintings point toward the botanical tradition. Yet the objects are not remarkable and as an archive there is really nothing to be learned or studied. And so while the statement "this is a feather" is true, the paintings leave the tether of "what kind?" and "why?" unfastened.

An archive of paintings and a book of poetry joined by a practice of walking and divided by form and materiality. I dreamt of a space that would house them both. Here is one blueprint for such a space:

When exhibited each painting's number corresponds to a couplet or line in *SPEECH*. Those lines become painting titles. This hinges the numbers to the book with the paintings in the middle: an odd bibliography. Viewers pick up a map of numbers and titles: a gallery-map-as-poem, a mobile didactic. As they walk, look, and read, they re-compose *SPEECH*, moving at their own pace and along unpredictable pathways. So, too, with a city and with a book whose streets and page numbers nudge readers in a certain direction. The book's architecture—the double-page spread that opens as the reader holds front and back covers—implies a beginning, middle, and end. Yet this structure can be subverted by reader sovereignty at any time. And the one who walks in the city vectors across the city plan at will. This uncertainty, borne of sovereignty, adds extra vibration to an already-vibrating citational space where language is framed by page boundaries and by front and back covers.

The subject who won't be indexed precisely and who makes place where self-indexing is relational, various, and repetitive, also makes paintings from this practice and from the objects of her context. Why not add the disciplinary divide between text and image to her collection of borders crossed?

A second blueprint:

Traces of the archive work their way into the book. First it was the writer and now it is the reader who finds a thing to pick up and inspect: feather, brick, twig, words, book. They take the ordinary thing into their home where home is inside and outside, present and past, made and remade: parts of *SPEECH*.

Sources

The following texts, artworks, and articulations were absorbed by and occasionally surface in the citational space that is *SPEECH*:

"Abu Dhabi Forms and Fragments: Muslim Space and the Modern City" by Mohamed El-Amrousi and John Biln; "All for You" sung by Ms. Eupheme Cooper, from The Library of Congress Endangered Music Project: The Arthur S. Alberts Collection; "Al Madhafah: The Living Room Performance" by Sandi Hilal as part of the "Permanent Temporariness: Sandi Hilal and Alessandro Petti" exhibition at the NYUAD Art Gallery 2018; "Art, Performance and Social Practice" class project at New York University Abu Dhabi, taught by Debra Levine; "AT THE RISK OF THE REAL" an installation by Cinthia Marcelle at the Sharjah Biennial 2015; *City Gates* by Elias Khoury; *Cosmopolitanism: Ethics in a World of Strangers* by Kwame Anthony Appiah; "A Crack in an Antarctic Ice Shelf Grew 17 Miles in the Last Two Months" by Jugal K. Patel, *The New York Times*; "Crime in Chicago: What Does the Research Tell Us?" published by the Institute for Policy Research at Northwestern University; *Crowd and not evening or light* by Leslie Scalapino; *Culture of One* by Alice Notley; "Disjuncture and Difference in the Global Cultural Economy" by Arjun Appadurai in *The Cultural Studies Reader* 3rd edition; *Do Muslim Women Need Saving?* by Lila Abu-Lughod; "Drawing Threads from Sight to Site" by Victoria Mitchell in *Textile* Volume 4, Issue 3; *Economies of Abandonment: Social Belonging and Endurance in Late Liberalism* and *The Empire of Love: Toward a Theory of Intimacy, Genealogy, and Carnality* by Elizabeth A. Povinelli; *From Civil Rights to Human Rights: Martin Luther King, Jr., and the Struggle for Economic Justice* by Thomas F. Jackson; *I, Lalla: The Poems of Lal Ded*, translated by Ranjit Hoskote; *Impossible Citizens: Dubai's Indian Diaspora* by Neha Vora; *The Impossible Indian: Gandhi and the Temptation of Violence* by Faisal Devji; *Migrant Labour in the Persian Gulf*, Mehran Kamrava and Zahra Babar, Eds.; "Overgrowth 9," a dress made only of sleeves, design and drawing by Lucy Leith; *The Performance of Becoming Human* by Daniel Borzutzky; "Police-

Recorded Crime and Disparities in Obesity & Blood Pressure Status in Chicago" published in the *Journal of the American Heart Association*; *Reconciliation: Islam, Democracy, and the West* by Benazir Bhutto; "Refugees and im/migrants," virtual issue of the *American Ethnologist*, Heide Castañeda, Seth M. Holmes, Annastiina Kallius, and Daniel Monterescu, Eds.; *Reinterpreting Menopause: Cultural and Philosophical Issues,* edited by Paul A. Komesaroff, Philipa Rothfield, and Jeanne Daly; "Somebody Blew Up America" by Amiri Baraka; "Sous Les Pavés La Plage" a sculpture and installation by Jonny Farrow; *Stress and Freedom* by Peter Sloterdijk; *Supple Science: A Robert Kocik Reader*; *Temporary People* by Deepak Unnikrishnan; "Totes Haus ur" an installation by Gregor Schneider; *The Undercommons: Fugitive Planning & Black Study* by Stefano Harney & Fred Moten; *The Universal Machine* by Fred Moten; "Varnam" a dance/video installation by Padmini Chettur at the Kochi Biennale 2016; "Wake Up America!" a speech by Dennis Kucinich; "Walking in the City" by Michel de Certeau from *The Practice of Everyday Life*; *Walking with the Comrades* by Arundhati Roy; "Where the sidewalk ends" a lecture by Yasser Elsheshtawy at the NYUAD Institute 2012; "Why Do Ladies Sing the Blues? Indigo Dyeing, Cloth Production, and Gender Symbolism in Kodi" by Janet Hoskins in *Cloth and Human Experience*; "Why Killer Whales Go Through Menopause" by Steph Yin, *The New York Times*; "World Poll" an interactive installation by Hans Haacke; "Your Day Is My Night" a film by Lynne Sachs; and, finally, my own "Climacteric" contribution to *Counter-desecration: A Glossary for Writing Within the Anthropocene*, "Compass & Hem," an unpublished manuscript, "Overcoding Class, Version 2," a poem published in *Columbia Poetry Review* 2013, and "Portable Horizons," a solo exhibition at Tashkeel gallery, Dubai.

Excerpts of *SPEECH* have been published as a chapbook from Hostile Books, as a "digitally degrading" version of the chapbook for *NANO* and in collaboration with Pierre Depaz, as a broadside by Amber McMillan for The Center for Book Arts in New York City, and in the following journals: *Opon, Humanities, The Boston Review, Canvas Middle East, Phoebe,* and *Tupelo Quarterly.* Thanks to those editors, artists, and publishers for their support and collaboration.

Jonny Farrow, Jennifer Firestone, Sarah Tarkanay, and Jacob Victorine read versions of this work along the way and I am grateful for their generous feedback. Deep gratitude to Stephen Motika for his attentive editing. Finally, I want to thank Kate Smith, Norman Kennedy, and everyone at The Marshfield School of Weaving where I learned the rhythms that in/form this book.

SPEECH makes a fictional space. Any resemblance to actual people and incidents is not intentional.

Jill Magi works in text, image, and textile and her books include *Threads, Torchwood, SLOT, Cadastral Map, LABOR, SIGN CLIMACTERIC,* and a monograph on text-image entitled *Pageviews/Innervisions.* Recent work has appeared in *Best American Experimental Writing* 2018, *Boston Review, Tupelo Quarterly, Phoebe,* and *Rivulet.* In October of 2017 Jill blogged for The Poetry Foundation, and in the spring of 2015 Jill wrote weekly commentaries for *Jacket2* on "a textile poetics." Her essays have appeared in *The Edinburgh Companion to the Critical Medical Humanities, The Force of What's Possible: Accessibility & the Avant-garde, The Racial Imaginary: Writers on Race in the Life of the Mind,* and *The Eco-Language Reader.* Jill has been awarded residencies with the Lower Manhattan Cultural Council Workspace program, the Brooklyn Textile Arts Center, and has had solo shows with Tashkeel in Dubai and the Project Space Gallery at New York University Abu Dhabi. For her community-based publishing work, *Poets & Writers* magazine named her as among the most inspiring writers in the world in 2010.

000026

000027

NIGHTBOAT BOOKS

Nightboat Books, a nonprofit organization, seeks to develop audiences for writers whose work resists convention and transcends boundaries. We publish books rich with poignancy, intelligence, and risk. Please visit nightboat.org to learn about our titles and how you can support our future publications.

The following individuals have supported the publication of this book. We thank them for their generosity and commitment to the mission of Nightboat Books:

Kazim Ali
Anonymous
Jean C. Ballantyne
Photios Giovanis
Amanda Greenberger
Anne Marie Macari
Elizabeth Motika
Benjamin Taylor
Jerrie Whitfield & Richard Motika

Nightboat Books gratefully acknowledges support from the National Endowment for the Arts.